Completely Prepared™

A Legacy of Caring™
Completely prepared guides for your life

WILL AND TRUST COMPANION GUIDE

Name: _____

Date: _____

Will and Trust Companion Guide

FIRST PRINTING, 2014
ISBN: 978-1496057280

Authored by Petersen, Kenneth C. & Smith, Shawn V.
Original bird concept logo design by Rachel Smith
Graphic design by BumbleBee Marketing Services
Cover design by Dee Renfro
Cover photos purchased from iStockPhoto

For ordering information please visit our website at www.completelyprepared.com

Printed in the United States of America

Completely Prepared
A Legacy of Caring
Completely prepared guides for your life

To our Valued Customers:

Thank you for choosing "Will and Trust Companion Guide" - the perfect companion document to your existing Will and Trust. Even if you don't have a Will or a Trust this guide will be valuable for organizing your existing records.

Why a companion document? In most Wills and Trusts many important personal records are not included. Instead of having your heirs search for this information, we created this guide to help complete the picture.

Help using this guide – For your convenience, we have placed these informative pages in the latter part of the guide so that your information will be prominently displayed in the front.

This guide is available both in a booklet form and also as a downloadable, fillable document from our website at www.completelyprepared.com. **If you would like to download a copy of our fillable form, please use the code WT50 for a 50% discount.**

Once again, thank you for choosing "Will and Trust Companion Guide".

When you have an opportunity, please visit our website and provide us with your feedback.

Sincerely,

Shawn Smith   Ken Petersen

Completely Prepared, Inc.

TABLE OF CONTENTS

1	CHECKLIST	

Upon my passing, please utilize the following checklist below in finalizing my estate (Please note that this checklist is general and may not include every detail. This is not a legal guideline):

CHECK WHEN COMPLETED	DESCRIPTION	SECTION NUMBER
	Review my location of records.	2
	Please notify my personal contacts.	6
	Contact my professional contacts.	7
	Follow my final wishes and arrange my final services.	8
	During my final services, have someone watch my home.	-
	Follow my organ donation wishes (if applicable).	8
	Request ten original death certificates from the funeral home.	8
	Prepare my obituary. Publish in the newspaper and social media.	15
	Review my Will and Trust documents. Contact my Preparer.	2, 7
	Find my passwords and log-ins.	2
	Review my financial assets and liabilities.	9-13
	Notify my financial advisor.	7
	Inform Social Security.	18
	Contact my last employer regarding benefits.	7
	Examine the contents of my safe deposit box.	17
	Notify the post office, review mail.	-
	Please arrange care for my pets.	-
	Process my life insurance claims.	2
	Notify financial institutions.	9-13
	Inform insurance providers.	14
	Review my business interests.	3
	Verify that all assets have been transferred to the trust.	9-13
	Meet with a tax preparer to file estate taxes.	7
	Distribute gifts to my charities.	5
	Distribute my personal property.	16
	Review my other information.	21
	Transfer ownership of my vehicles.	20
	Pay all bills.	-
	Close card accounts.	4
	At my passing, arrange for appraisals on all properties.	19
	File trust tax return annually	-
	Thank you for taking care of my estate.	

A current list of important records is listed below (examples for "Location" include: A file cabinet, a fire proof file or safe, a safe deposit box, storage facility, etc.): The ways to access this information is also listed below (examples for "Access Information" include: A key, combination lock, a code, etc.):

TYPE	LOCATION	ACCESS INFORMATION
Address Book		
Adoption Papers (if applicable)		
Birth & Marriage Certificates		
Business Agreements		
Deeds		
Divorce Agreement (if applicable)		
Doctor Records		
Durable Power of Attorney for Finances		
Durable Power of Attorney for Healthcare		
Family Photos and Memorabilia		
Family Videos		
Health Care Directives		
Home Inventory List		
Life Insurance Policies		
Military Documents		
Organ Donation Instructions		
Passwords/Log-ins Book		
Prenuptial Agreement		
Product & Warranty Guides		
Tax Returns & Other Tax Records		
Wills & Trust Documents		
Other:		
Other:		
Other:		
Other:		
Other:		
Other:		

3	BUSINESS INTERESTS			

Business interest information is listed below: (Examples for "Type" include: Sole Proprietorships, Corporations, LLC's, General and Limited Partnerships)

TYPE	BUSINESS NAME	PERCENTAGE OF OWNERSHIP	LOCATION OF RECORDS

4	CARDS			

Current cards are listed below: (Examples for "Type" include: Credit cards, gas cards, debit cards, access cards, membership cards, other, etc.)

TYPE	COMPANY	PHONE NUMBER	LOCATION OF RECORDS

5	CHARITIES - LEGACY OF CARING			

Current Legacy of Caring™ gifts are listed below: (Examples for "Type" include: Non-profit organizations, schools, universities, colleges, charities, foundations, endowments, etc.)

TYPE	NAME OF CHARITY	% OF ESTATE OR AMOUNT	LOCATION OF RECORDS

6	CONTACTS - PERSONAL

If I have an address book containing the names of all of my personal contacts, this book is located here:
_____ .

If I do not have an address book, please see my personal contacts below that should be notified in the event of my death or incapacity: (Examples for "Type" include: Family, relatives, friends, and neighbors.)

TYPE	NAME	PHONE NUMBER	EMAIL ADDRESS

7	CONTACTS – PROFESSIONAL

Current professional contacts are listed below:

TYPE	NAME	PHONE NUMBER
Accountant / Tax preparer:		
Attorney:		
Bank officer:		
Business Associate:		
Clergy:		
Employer:		
Financial advisor:		
Health Care Provider:		
Investment broker:		
Insurance agent #1:		
Insurance agent #2:		
Physician:		
Veterinarian:		
Will and Trust Preparer:		
Other:		
Other:		

8	FINAL WISHES		

Current final wishes are listed below:

TYPE	ORGANIZATION NAME	PHONE NUMBER	LOCATION OF RECORDS
Religious Affiliation:			
Funeral home:			
Cemetery:			
Memorial park:			
Other:			

Funeral home (if prepaid) account number:	
Cemetery plot (if purchased) lot #, block #, section #:	
Casket company name/phone number (if prepaid) account #:	
Urn company name/phone number (if prepaid) account #:	
Instructions for casket or urn:	
Organ donation information:	
Clergy preferred:	
Memorial service location:	
Celebration of life service?	
Pall bearers:	
Flowers or donations in lieu of flowers:	
Special songs and/or scriptures:	
Special poems or stories:	
Preferred singer(s):	
Preferred instrumentals:	
Preferred speakers:	
Clothing or jewelry preference?	
Public viewing, private viewing or no viewing?	
Casket followed by burial, by cremation, cremation only?	
Open or closed casket?	
If cremation, what are your instructions for ashes?	
Memorial display Item:	
Location of photos:	
Other:	

9	FINANCIAL ASSETS – TRUST ASSETS

Trust assets are listed below: (Examples for "Type" include: Checking, banking, savings, credit union, money market, business checking, business savings, certificate of deposit, investment accounts, and savings bonds, etc.)

TYPE	FINANCIAL INSTITUTION	ACCOUNT NUMBER	LOCATION OF RECORDS

10	FINANCIAL ASSETS – NON-TRUST ASSETS

Non-trust assets are listed below: (Examples for "Type" include: Life insurance, annuities, 401(k)s, 403(b)s, Roth IRA's, and IRA's – Note: All proceeds shall pass to the recipient named as beneficiary with the institution listed. A beneficiary may be one or more individuals, a trust, or a charity, etc.)

TYPE	FINANCIAL INSTITUTION	ACCOUNT NUMBER	LOCATION OF RECORDS

11	FINANCIAL ASSETS – NOTES RECEIVABLE

PAYER	ORIGINAL NOTE AMOUNT	DUE DATE	SECURED (YES OR NO)	LOCATION OF RECORDS

12	FINANCIAL LIABILITIES

Financial liabilities are listed below: (Examples of "Type" include: Loans, mortgage balances, credit card balances, personal loans, delinquent taxes, installment loan balances, student loans, life insurance loans, personal unsecured loans, and retirement plan loans.)

TYPE	CREDITOR	PHONE NUMBER	LOCATION OF RECORDS

13	FINANCIAL LIABILITIES – NOTES PAYABLE

PAYEE	ORIGINAL NOTE AMOUNT	DUE DATE	SECURED (YES OR NO)	LOCATION OF RECORDS

14	INSURANCES

Current insurance providers are listed below: (Examples for "Type" include: Auto, boat, RV, airplane, motorcycle, travel, umbrella, liability, vision, professional liability, mortgage, personal property, rental property, earthquake, flood, home owner's, life, long-term care, medical, Medicare, Medicaid, Medigap, dental, disability, etc.)

TYPE	COMPANY NAME	PHONE NUMBER	LOCATION OF RECORDS

15	PERSONAL INFORMATION
Full name:	
Spouse/Partner's name:	
Full residence address:	
Home phone number:	
Mobile phone number:	
Work phone number:	
Email address(es):	
Birthdate:	
Birth place:	
Occupation:	
Father's name & place of birth:	
Mother's name & place of birth:	
Adoption agreement location:	
Birth certificate location:	
Citizenship papers location:	
Divorce certificate location (if applicable):	
Driver's license location:	
Marriage certificate location:	
Marriage date & place of marriage:	
Organ donor cards location:	
Passport location:	
Prenuptial agreement location:	
Social security card location:	
Social security number:	
Other:	
Other:	
Other:	
Other:	
Other:	
Other:	
Other:	

16	PERSONAL PROPERTY	

Personal properties are listed below: The following are wishes for gifting of personal items not included in my will or trust.

RECIPIENT'S NAME	ITEM DESCRIPTION	LOCATION OF ITEM

17	SAFE DEPOSIT BOX

Safe deposit box information is located below: (Examples of the contents may include: Stock certificates, coins, stamps, collectibles, vehicle titles, deeds, mortgages, original birth, marriage and death certificates, adoption papers, home inventory photos and video tapes, etc.)

Bank Name:	
Bank Address:	
Bank Phone Number:	
Box Number:	
Box Key Location:	
Authorized Persons:	
Notes:	

18	SOCIAL SECURITY INFORMATION

The Social Security Administration (SSA) website has information on survivor benefits. Their website is www.ssa.gov.

When I have passed away, contact the SSA by calling 1-800-772-1213 (or check the Internet for the most current phone number). They will provide instructions for canceling direct deposits and/or returning any checks to the SSA.

The SSA will pay a one-time lump sum death benefit to my surviving spouse, or if no surviving spouse this benefit can be paid to a surviving child.

The SSA will provide survivor's benefits to eligible family members. The SSA provides publications on the subject of Survivor's Benefits and Understanding Benefits.

Social security checks are mailed (Yes/No):	
Social security checks are direct deposited (Yes/No):	
Name of financial institution for direct deposit:	
Financial institution's full address:	
Financial institution's phone number:	
Financial institution's account number:	
Social security records location:	
Other:	
Other:	
Other:	
Other:	

19	REAL ESTATE	

Current real estate is listed below: (Examples of "Type" include: Land, single family residence, multi-family residence, commercial property, etc.)

TYPE	PROPERTY ADDRESS	LOCATION OF RECORDS

20	VEHICLES		

Current vehicles are listed below: (Examples for "Type" include: Cars, trucks, trucks, boats, RV's, airplanes, motorcycles, etc.)

TYPE	MAKE/MODEL/YEAR	LICENSE NUMBER	LOCATION OF RECORDS

21	OTHER INFORMATION	

Other information is listed below: (Examples for "Type" include: All items that did not fit into the other sections)

TYPE	DESCRIPTION	LOCATION OF RECORDS

i	# COMPANY INFORMATION

Contact Information:	**Completely Prepared, Inc.** Address: 5424 Sunol Blvd., Suite 10-121, Pleasanton, CA 94566 Phone: 800-468-9312 (please leave a message) Email: info@completelyprepared.com Website: www.completelyprepared.com Like us on Facebook: www.facebook.com/completelyprepared Follow us on Twitter: www.twitter.com/comprepared Check out our YouTube Channel: www.youtube.com/completelyprepared
Our Mission:	Our mission is to spread the word about personal organization and life planning to as many people as possible! We are committed to this goal and in helping you achieve optimum records organization through our concise and easy-to-use guides.
Our Company:	Ken Petersen and Shawn Smith have a passion for helping others with personal organizing and life planning. Similar to the experiences that many others have had, they had family members pass away without a plan and no legacy left behind. They rallied with their loved ones to organize final details and search for needed important information, an arduous task especially during a family crisis. Ken and Shawn made it their life goal to be completely prepared with their own personal records so that their families would not be left to search for their information. They were determined to leave a Legacy of Caring™. Wishing to share this with others, they developed the easy to use and concise *Will and Trust Companion Guide* and *My Estate Records Guide* which organizes all of your important records in one place. Also in an effort to help people find their passion in life, Ken has mentored hundreds of people in the area of life planning. If you need to find your passion, download *My Life Planning Guide* from our website and put yourself on the right track to a happy life!
Ken Petersen, Founder	Over the past 25 years, Ken has mentored couples and singles in the area of personal organization and life planning. Ken is also well-known for his commitment to training and education both personally and professionally.
Shawn Smith, Founder	Shawn Smith is an expert in business and personal organization techniques and content writing. She has over 30 years of experience working for large and mid-sized firms assisting top executives in all aspects of business organization. Wanting to take her expertise to the public, she teamed up with her business partner and former co-worker, Ken Petersen, to create the most concise and easy to use guides possible for personal organization and life planning.

ii	LEGAL DISCLAIMER AND TERMS OF USE
Information Not Legal Advice:	This document has been prepared for general information purposes only and should not be considered legal advice. Legal advice is dependent upon the specific circumstances of each situation. Therefore, the information contained in this document cannot replace the advice of competent legal counsel licensed in your state.
Website:	Our website, www.completelyprepared.com, contains links to other resources on the Internet. Those links are provided as citations and aids to help you identify and locate other Internet resources that may be of interest, and are not intended to state or imply that we sponsor or are affiliated or associated with the persons or entities who created those sites, nor are the links intended to state or imply that we are legally authorized to use any trade name, registered trademark, logo, legal or official seal, or copyright symbol that may be reflected in the links.
Email:	Sending an email message to Completely Prepared™, Inc. staff does not create an attorney-client relationship between Completely Prepared™, Inc. and you. Sending email to an attorney or other service mentioned in this site does NOT create an attorney-client relationship between you and the attorney. Unless you are already a client of the attorney, your email may NOT be protected by the attorney-client privilege. Moreover, unless it is encrypted, email can be intercepted by persons other than the recipient.
Document Security:	When using the downloadable version of this guide, we cannot be held liable for document security. We can only suggest that you password protect and/or encrypt your files to maintain the highest possible security. We also suggest that you maintain a back-up file on a USB flash drive or CD-ROM in case your computer crashes. You should always take precautions by using highly rated virus protection software.

The Reason:	This document represents a snapshot of your estate records each time you update it. It is beneficial to your loved ones or trusted friends to have all of your data located in one place. With this document, along with your Will and Trust, your legacy and the location of your estate records will be known.
Why Should You Be Completely Prepared?	"Will and Trust Companion Guide" will help you be completely prepared by providing you a place to store or list important information not covered in your Will or Trust. This guide represents a snapshot of your records. Not only will it keep your records organized throughout your life, "Will and Trust Companion Guide" along with your Will and Trust, will likely be the most important resource for your family when the inevitable happens. Being Completely Prepared™ is one of the greatest gifts you can give to your family. You never know when the inevitable will happen. The undeniable truth is that you could be young, middle-aged or golden-aged. Therefore, it is important to spend time now completing "Will and Trust Companion Guide". It will provide vital information and guidance to your family. By keeping your information up-to-date, you also leave a blueprint of your estate records. Over the course of time, we have all seen and read about people who were not prepared and did not have their affairs in order. In fact, MOST of us fall into that category! The task of organizing our records feels overwhelming; and it can be time consuming to collect all the data and then periodically spend time to keep it updated. However, if your estate records location is not known, heirs will be hampered in their efforts to handle the difficult affairs involved in reconciling your estate. It could take your family months to go through all of your paperwork and records. When several heirs are involved, it can be difficult to decide who will take charge. If you are prepared and organized, imagine the relief your family will feel to know that your loving care has provided them with this guide. We call this "A Legacy of Caring™", the cornerstone of our philosophy. Those who have been designated to carry out and honor final wishes will be extremely grateful that this completed guide was prepared and kept up-to-date.
Making Changes to Your Guide (downloadable and booklet versions):	If you are filling this in on your computer, and when you open the document in Adobe®Reader®, you can utilize the bookmarks available to easily move from section-to-section in order to quickly make any changes to your data. Be sure to save your changes. If you are using the booklet version, you may want to consider filling this in using a pencil so that you can make changes to it as needed. We suggest that you keep this guide with your Will and Trust for a complete set of documents.

Protecting Your Guide (downloadable version):	If you choose to fill this in on your computer, we recommend that you have a reliable security software program and/or firewall to protect the information on your computer, and we also recommend that you utilize strong passwords (using a combination of letters, numbers, and symbols) when saving your document. This guide can also be filled in on your mobile device. If you have filled in this guide on your computer, we highly recommend that you take steps to password protect it. For an on-line tutorial, check this video: http://acrobatusers.com/tutorials/how-do-i-password-protect-a-document. If the video is no longer available, go to your on-line search engine and type: "How to password protect a PDF document". You'll find a great deal of information on how to do this on the Internet.
Printing Your Guide (downloadable version):	If you'd like, you can print out your downloadable guide. You can print only the sections that apply to you, or you can print the entire guide. You can print the pages you have filled in, or you can print blank copies of the guide which will give you the freedom to fill in the guide by hand or with a typewriter.
Storing Your Guide (downloadable and booklet versions):	Due to the sensitive nature of the information contained in this guide, we recommend that you store this guide in a secure location such as a safe or fireproof file. IMPORTANT: Once you have completed this guide, make sure your executor or responsible family member is provided with access instructions so they can locate this guide in the event you pass away unexpectedly or become incapacitated. Note: If you store this in a safe deposit box, it will be much more difficult for your trusted person to gain access to your guide. For the downloadable version, we recommend two options: *Option 1:* You can store the guide on a flash-drive (no need to print it out). You can also scan other important related documents to add to your computer file and flash drive. *Option 2:* If you'd rather print it out, you can 3-hole punch and place it in a binder with an index tab for each section to keep it organized. You can also add sheet protectors so that you can insert examples of interesting things relating to the various sections or include other important documents in order to keep everything in one place. For the booklet version, we recommend that you place it in an accordion file with flap, Place your booklet in the front, and then you can place other important documents behind it, keeping everything together in one place. Again, we recommend that this guide along with your Will and Trust be stored together.

NOTES

Will and Trust Companion Guide

NOTES

NOTES

NOTES

Will and Trust Companion Guide

NOTES